Identity
What It Means
To Be
You

Kriss Mitchell ND, M.Ed

This book and all other books, articles and audio CDs written by Kristine I Mitchell, can be found on the Living Well Counseling and Consulting, LLC website — www.livingwellcc.com

For information about permission to reproduce selections from this book, please write to:
Kriss Mitchell, ND, M.Ed
Living Well Counseling and Consulting, LLC
761 N Thornton St., Suite C
Post Falls, ID 83854
Or email

livingwellcc@gmail.com

DEDICATION

This book is dedicated to my daughters, Dorey and Faith.

They have been an inspiration to me to find wisdom in all I do.

I love you both so much!

CONTENTS

ACKNOWLEDGMENTS

I would like to acknowledge my wonderful editor, Mark Sandford, M.Div, who helped me shape this book into what it is today. My talented graphic artist Brandon Loken picked exactly the right cover art for me. His talent in helping to format what I have written is amazing and greatly appreciated.

My daughter Faith Mitchell, who we lovingly call our "grammar nazi" helped me edit the book along the way for grammar and word changes. Her patience and encouragement was invaluable.

There are more people than I can list who have, in one form or another, inspired what is on the pages of this book. I have learned so much from my experiences in the counseling room, with people who have trusted me to speak into their lives. Thank you all for making this project into a reality!

1 CHAPTER

THE BLUEPRINT THAT IS YOU

I see a very common response in the counseling office when I mention the word, *"Identity."* I get a blank look, an "uh huh," and the conversation moves on. Over the years, I've learned to work with that response and allow my clients the time to explore what identity means. The message of identity keeps being reinforced as a significant issue in the lives of many of the people I speak with. It is clear that lack of identity is a much bigger problem than people think it is. I describe it as an epidemic of our culture. We are taught to have roles and jobs, which then become what we are, and determine our value as human beings. We don't hear the truth, which is: *we are not what we do.* We are unique individuals who perform certain functions, but those functions don't define us — we define the functions.

I have believed for a long time that identity is what can be called that unique "blueprint" from which the Lord created us. This blueprint is who we are. Not who we are in Christ, which is another thing, but who we *are*. Male or female, blonde or brunette, blue eyes or brown eyes — even down to the preferences for the food we like to eat, what we consider delightful, and what makes us curl back with fear or disgust. As human beings, we are individuals with a complex compilation of attributes organized in a distinctive way that, as an end result, becomes me and you and your neighbor and all the people who have made up and presently make up our world. It is hard to believe that, in all these millions of people, there is not one who is the same as another!

Identity in Christ vs personal identity

When we talk about identity, people often think that what is being referred to is our identity in Christ. For the purposes of this book, that is not the case. Personal identity is the creative gift of God to us. Identity in Christ is a positional term used to describe the "benefits" secured for each of us through the death and resurrection of Jesus Christ. These benefits are given to any person who believes in the Lord Jesus Christ as their Savior. Our personal identities are different — they are unique to each one of us, and are comprised of our personality, our gifts, our talents, body style, and many other things, which in turn give us significant clues to our purpose in life. For example, someone who is 6'5", with a heavy frame and musculature, would probably not be well suited as a dancer or gymnast. A dancer's or gymnast's body style is quite different from that of a person who would be better suited as a football player or a logger. Someone with a quiet persona, who would rather research information and write about it, may not be comfortable as a public speaker.

Some people have come to believe dying to self means they must die to who they are as a person in order that Christ may live in them. Paul did not say that. He said:

> **Galatians 2:20, NKJV:** *I am crucified with Christ, nevertheless I live; yet not I but Christ who lives in me: and the life which I now live in the flesh I live by the faith of the Son of God, who loved me and gave himself for me*

The sense of this verse is that we are to crucify the sinful desires which keep us from following Christ and keep His nature from manifesting through us. We are, with His help, bringing to death carnal inclinations that oppose Him. But we must not forget the part of the verse that says —NEVERTHELESS, I Live! Christ lives within us, and we are to reflect His love, His beauty, His compassion and His grace through our own unique and wonderful body, soul and personal spirit.

> **Psalm 139:13-16, Amp.** — *For You formed my inward parts; You wove me in my mother's*

womb. I will give thanks to You, for I am fearfully and wonderfully made; wonderful are Your works, And my soul knows it very well. My frame was not hidden from You, when I was made in secret, [and] skillfully wrought in the depths of the earth; Your eyes have seen my unformed substance; and in Your book were all written the days that were ordained [for me] when as yet there was not one of them.

Does this verse sound like it is describing a master craftsman or a production line? If God did not build into us a unique design, what would be the need for Proverbs 22:6? (*Train up a child in the way he should go.* In the Hebrew, the meaning is that we should train up a child according to his own natural bent.) Why would He need to make sure we knew to look for how He made our children, and to direct them towards that?

Our identity in Christ is positional. It is an identity that we share with every other person in the body of Christ. Our personal identity, which is the focus of this discussion, is unique and belongs to us alone.

JOURNAL ACTIVITY:

1. ***What does personal identity mean to you?***

2 CHAPTER

OUR PERSONAL PERSPECTIVE

As anyone who has lost their way in life can attest, there are significant obstacles to accepting or developing the authentic self. The very society we live in tends to erode individuality and promote the idea that there is only one concept of the ideal self. It is communicated to us through subtle and not-so-subtle ways that a person must fit into a certain profile to be successful, beautiful, or noticed in certain social circles. People who are considered different can often find themselves pushed to the fringes of society, and becoming onlookers rather than participants in their own lives. In reality, being different is not a disadvantage; it is all in how people sees themselves. There are people who haven't fit the profile who have been very successful in society. How have they defied the odds and risen above their perceived obstacles? More often than not, they have accepted themselves for who they are. They have had a vision for their life and have not let people or circumstances dictate their outcomes.

If we look through the lens of attachment theory, we see that very young children have several crucial jobs to perform within the first year of life. They must answer two questions — the first being, "Am I worthy of love?" and the second, "Can I trust you to meet my needs?" Attempting to answer these creates the first measurable obstacle. Developmentally, children are somewhat ill equipped to answer, simply because their level of reasoning is limited. Their world is very small, and they have limited life experience. Furthermore, they don't understand the social nuances a person needs to comprehend in order to empathize or recognize the *big picture* of life.

Answering these two questions should be relatively simple, shouldn't it? For an adult, maybe; what complicates the process is that the answers usually come within the first year or two of life. The way a child answers them will have significant implications as to how the child sees life in general and how they respond to it as they grow and mature. How these questions are answered will reflect dramatically on how the child accepts and sees self in relation to those who surround them in their families, careers, and social lives. It seems as though questions that have such magnitude should not be left in the hands of an infant or toddler. The good news is that, in essence, they are not the child's sole

Handwritten margin notes (left): My Mom was all about looks + personality; I fell short - Not beautiful, smart or talented. Hedy Lamarr Paulette Goddard 5 bad marriages

Handwritten margin notes (right): I wasn't worthy of love or acceptance; I wasn't special. Shirley Temple was the criteria + I didn't come close. She was the same age as my Mom/born 1928

Handwritten notes (bottom): My Mom loved hollywood stars Joan Crawford Ginger Rogers Myra Loy Vivien Leigh Rita Hayworth Jean Harlow responsibility to answer, but the child does have the final say. Parents and siblings have a very large impact on how these questions are answered. The experience and perception of the child facing this great unknown quantity is, to a large degree, the foundation of how they are answered and applied to the rest of the child's life.

Our society has a tendency to erode our perspectives with regard to what is true about each of us. For example, individuals who grew up in homes where the overarching philosophy was, "children are to be seen and not heard," learned, among other things, that, "My opinions don't matter;" "No one listens to me;" "My feelings don't matter," and, "I don't matter." If we decide, based on those conclusions, that *as an individual* we have no value, then we are left with a belief that we are valuable only *because of what we do.* Through that lens, our value wavers with every passing opinion, and we have little inner strength to maintain the integrity of the creation God envisioned as He developed our blueprint. What, deep inside, we know to be true about ourselves, is considered wrong in our own minds, but we are the very individuals who should know firsthand what the truth is!

The optimum perspective an emotionally healthy child develops is that he or she is loveable and that other people are trustworthy enough to meet their needs. Human beings see examples of this every day in their pets. Pets usually don't perform any type of function. We love them and take care of them simply because we have chosen to bring them into our homes. In my house, I have a cat that is wonderfully dear to my heart, and he doesn't have to do anything but be around in order for me to feel this way about him. That is what it is like to be loved just because you exist.

In order for children to develop this perspective, their experience in life should be similar. Children's self-worth is formed around the experience they have in the world that surrounds them. What that world may look like to a young child is that parents will respond in loving and healthy ways to needs and mistakes. Parents respond either by saying yes or no. They affirm their love for the child. Their discipline separates who the child is from what the child has done. In these ways, the child learns over time that parents consider them to be loveable no matter what they do. Additionally, the child learns that sometimes they do things that are not appropriate and those behaviors need to be corrected; but in no way does the behavior increase or decrease how much the child is loved.

It is important to establish that this book is not meant to parent-bash. Parents make mistakes because their parents made mistakes, and we are all products of environments that were modeled for us growing up. As individuals, we are not responsible for how our parents raised us, but we are responsible for how we have responded to what our parents have done. This includes how we have judged them, what we have decided about the mistakes they have made, how grateful we are for the good things they have done, and how we manage our relationships with them. It also includes what belief systems we incorporate into our lives in response to childhood experiences. There does come a point when we take responsibility for our lives, stop blaming our parents for their mistakes, and get the help we need to move forward in a healthy manner if the fruit of our lives is not as good as we would like it to be.

Our parents can't teach us what they didn't learn themselves, so most often what happens is one of three scenarios. First, if we decide that we can trust other people but are not worthy to receive love just because we exist, we will decide to trust whatever those around us say about us, because we consider our own opinions to be in error. This decision often comes from the confusion children feel when feelings are not validated. For example, a child wakes up in the night and is scared, thinking there is something under the bed. The child may be told, "Honey, there is no reason for you to be scared; there is nothing under your bed. You are safe, so go back to sleep." Does the parent intentionally set out to invalidate the child? Absolutely not! Unfortunately, if that message is sent over and over again, the child will learn that they cannot trust their feelings because someone they trust has contradicted what they are feeling. Significant agitation arises, and in order for the child not to live in a state of perpetual confusion, they decide to disregard their feelings, discount and ignore them.

What the parent said was absolutely true, wasn't it? There was nothing under the bed, and there was no reason for the child to be scared. However, the child was *feeling* scared. It is important to first acknowledge the way a person *is* feeling, and then help them figure out whether or not it is valid — we don't just dismiss the feeling. That is called invalidation, and it sends the message that what the other person is feeling isn't what they should be feeling.

As parents consistently fail to acknowledge the opinions their children express, other situations can arise in which the same message is communicated. In abusive situations, children may be punished for expressing their feelings, thoughts or opinions. Abusive parents send a message that the child can't do anything right — that no matter what they do, they can't please the parents. A belief system starts to develop around perfection. Perfection then becomes the child's goal, because in their mind, if they are perfect, then they will have all the bases covered. What this can eventually look like in adult life is a person who isn't able to believe in him or herself, and only feels good or successful when others validate their work, praise them for whatever they might be doing at the time, or include them in group activities. The person believes that they need to strive for perfection because if they perform perfectly, they will always meet expectations and be successful.

2. A second scenario results from deciding that we can trust ourselves, and that we are worthy to be loved, but that we can't trust other people. A person may reach these conclusions because over time significant people in their lives are either abusive or

11

don't prove themselves trustworthy. The person who believes they can't trust others has been let down over and over, or they haven't been responded to when they needed something. In a family situation, this can result when parents:

Have substance abuse issues

✳ *Have forms of mental illness that go untreated or unrecognized*

✶ *Are simply neglectful; consistently putting their careers, wants, or desires ahead of their families*

From these forms of neglect, the child learns that no one is there for them. It appears to the child that they can't count on others, so a belief develops that if they want something done, or need something, they have to provide it for themselves. Often these individuals can have bonding issues or problems with being vulnerable and emotionally available with intimate partners. These are the adults who appear very self-sufficient and are not very emotionally open. Bottom line, they simply don't need anyone else. They are often very gifted and have above-average skills, so they can provide for themselves in the areas that are important to them. They may also be quite manipulative, because if people can't be trusted, they need to manipulate or control to get what they want.

3. A third scenario, which is the most problematic, is one in which children decide they can't trust themselves — that they aren't valuable enough to be loved in and of themselves, but they can't trust other people either. This is usually the consequence of much trauma, neglect, or abuse, consistent over time. When such a child grows up, being in relationship with him or her feels like a constant cycle of "come here/go away, come here/go away." Relationships are very difficult, if not impossible, with one who has this type of belief system, and he or she tends to highly frustrate others around them.

No matter which of these three scenarios is ours, as we grow and change, we search for the blessing. We concentrate on what we consider to be the important things in life — security, love, success, and beauty, and we search for what works. As we grow, we develop defense mechanisms and personality quirks that we believe will get us what we want and need in life. In the pursuit of those things, the degree to which we yield to unhealthy and untrue beliefs about ourselves and our surroundings is the degree to which our idea of who we are becomes more and more distorted. It can become so distorted that we are unable to see the truth about ourselves, and we get lost. We lose our way, and end up on a path that is not ours to walk. As we get farther and farther away from our true selves, we move into higher levels of stress and strife. Our eyes move from a true vision for our lives to simply existing, surviving and worrying about how to support ourselves, how to be acceptable to others, and how to increase the self-worth that we believe we do not have.

As we go, we create facades that we decide are more acceptable than how we see ourselves. We do our best to maintain those facades because if people really knew who we were, they wouldn't like us. We determine that perfection is the goal, and that the closer we can move to that standard, the more success, security or love we will have. Our focus becomes how to get more of these *things* to fill the empty places in our lives. Life becomes all about doing and surviving, rather than just being.

When wounds go deep, it takes time to sort through the flotsam and jetsam of our lives and decide what is true. *"Who* am I?" That is the important question that we need to answer. However, all too often, we answer by asking, "*What* am I?" or by giving a detailed resume that trumpets what we *do*. But remember, what we do is not who we are, and that concept may be very overwhelming to some. It is an idea that you may need to think about for a while.

JOURNAL ACTIVITY:

1. *Are you worthy to be loved?*
2. *Can you trust others to meet your needs?*
3. *Where have you been invalidated in your life?*

3 CHAPTER

THE POWER OF BELIEF

Because we have been discussing belief systems, before we go any farther, it would be prudent to discuss belief and why it is so powerful in our lives. As discussed in the last chapter, deep seated belief systems a child develops will affect how they live their life as an adult. Why is that true?

Over the last few years, we have heard much about the subject of belief. Some of that talk centers on the idea that if we believe for things or resources, those things will come to us. Years ago, Christians heard Oral Roberts and the Word of Faith movement talk about this, calling it *Seed Faith*. This concept has been around for a very long time in one form or another. The difference today is that along with the age-old idea of "positive thinking," a discussion of quantum physics is lending a little more credence to the subject. There have also been studies done in the area of Positive Psychology that show conclusively the positive effects of joy, happiness, and positive thought on our physical bodies, as well as on the quality of our lives. People who have a more positive belief system are happier, healthier and more productive.

When it comes to belief, more often than not, these kinds of ideas are often married with a spiritualistic agenda that to most Christians is distasteful. However, although truth and error are often combined, we don't want to throw the baby out with the bathwater. Belief is foundational to the Christian walk. Scripture teaches us to "believe unto salvation" — if we believe we will receive. So, what is it that is true, and what is the error that we need to throw away? Let's look at Scripture to find out: Mark 9:23, NKJV — *And Jesus said to him, "If you can believe? All things are possible to him who believes"* (in this verse, Jesus is responding to the young boy with the deaf and dumb spirit).

Rick Renner says in his book, *Sparkling Gems from the Greek*:

"The word 'possible' is the Greek word, *dunata*....It expresses the idea of ability, power, one who is able and capable, or one who is competent. This scripture emphatically tells us that there is a power that causes one to become able, capable, or competent for any task. When this power comes on the scene and begins to operate in an individual's life, it doesn't matter how unfit or unqualified he was before; this power energizes him and makes him capable for the task.

But who is this person who can accomplish impossible feats? Jesus said that all things are possible to him "who believes." The word, "believes," is the Greek word pisteuonti, from the word pistis, the Greek word for faith. However, when pistis becomes pisteuonti, as in this verse, it pictures a person who is believing. This is not someone who once had an experience of faith in the past; rather, this is a person who is presently believing right now. His faith is actively reaching forward right now to grab hold of what God has promised."

Matthew 21:22 says: *And all things you ask in prayer, believing, you will receive.* Here, the same word, *pisteuo,* has been translated, *"believing."*

Mark 5:35-43 — *While He was still speaking, they came from the house of the synagogue official, saying, "Your daughter has died; why trouble the Teacher anymore?" But Jesus, overhearing what was being spoken, said to the synagogue official, "Do not be afraid any longer; only believe." And He allowed no one to accompany Him, except Peter and James and John the brother of James. They came to the house of the synagogue official; and He saw a commotion, and people loudly weeping and wailing. And entering in, He said to them, "Why make a commotion and weep? The child has not died, but is* *asleep.*"

Notice that Jesus instructed the official to believe. He didn't tell him to pray or worship; Jesus simply wanted his heartfelt belief.

Mark 11:23 — *Truly I say to you, whoever says to this mountain, "Be taken up and cast into the sea," and does not doubt in his heart, but believes that what he says is going to happen, it will be granted him.*

The Greek word here for "heart" is *kardia*, from which we derive the word, "cardiac," referencing the heart. And in this verse, "believes," in Greek is the same word we saw in Mark 9:23 — *pisteuo*. The Scriptures not only makes reference to the heart as a physical organ, but as the center of spiritual life, and thus, the engine of spiritual belief.

Belief is not only spiritual, but it is also chemical, a combination of thought and emotion, the powerful place of agreement between the brain and the heart. By contrast, when we merely think about something, there usually is little or no emotional charge connected with it. We see a spider on the wall and think that it may be a good idea to remove it from the house. We either act on it, or we don't. But someone else might see that spider and have a panic attack, because as a child they woke up one night with a large spider in their bed. The memory of the spider was married with the emotion of fear, which produced a far more powerful reaction, and led to the belief that spiders are horrid, and they must get away from them at all costs. This belief became so strong that the physical body reacts violently to it. The brain and heart have come together in a place of agreement about spiders, and a powerful belief has been created.

Studies from many university hospitals around the nation have shown that the heart and brain both produce electro-magnetic fields around the body as well as measurable frequencies and vibrations which affect the world around them. According to the HeartMath Institute, the electromagnetic field of the heart is "five thousand times greater in strength than the field produced by the brain." This field is measurable up to ten feet from the body, but is thought to extend up to a mile (*The HeartMath Solution*, p. 33)! This makes sense in light of our example above. Thought produced by the brain is much less powerful than belief produced by the heart. When the two are brought together, the belief has much more power than the thought alone.

According to HeartMath: "An electromagnetic field is just that: magnetic…The emotional resonance you send out from your heart rhythms is like a magnet, attracting people, situations, and opportunities. When you're in a state of appreciation, your energy is more buoyant and spirited. You feel better mentally, emotionally and physically."

Scripture preceded science; Matthew 7:1-2, NKJV, says, *Judge not, that you be not judged. For with what judgment you judge, you will be judged;*

and with the measure you use, it will be measured back to you. God so designs us that we tend to attract what our heart believes is true. Studies at HeartMath Institute have shown that in developing an attitude of thankfulness and appreciation, our nervous system comes into balance — our heart beats in a coherent rhythm, and the two main branches of our autonomic nervous system are synchronized. It is consistent throughout God's creation that anything that is synchronized and in balance is more efficient and more effective.

Scripture gives us at least 108 verses that mention "thanks," and it specifically lists things to be thankful for. There are many verses in the Psalms that say things like, *give thanks to the Lord, His loving kindness extends forever,* or *I will give thanks to the Lord with all my heart!* The Lord is showing us things we can be thankful for, if we can't come up with them on our own.

God is a God who absolutely wants to bless us, and within our physical bodies, He created the means by which we can receive those blessings. In His word, He speaks to us about how to be in position to receive everything He has for us:

Philippians 4:6-8, NKJV — *Be anxious for nothing, but in everything, by prayer and supplication, with thanksgiving, let your requests be made known to God; and the peace of God, which surpasses every understanding, shall guard your hearts and your thoughts by Christ Jesus. Finally, brethren, whatever is true, whatever is honorable,* *whatever is right, whatever is pure, whatever is lovely, whatever is of good repute, if there is any excellence and if anything worthy of praise, dwell on these things.*

The Greek word translated, "dwell," in this verse is *logizomai*. This word deals with reality. If I think (*logizomai*), or reckon, that my garden does not have weeds in it when the reality is that that it does, this is not truly *logizomai*; it is pretending or deceiving myself. This word refers to facts, not suppositions. Elsewhere in the Bible, this same word is translated, "think," "reason," and "suppose," among other meanings. We *think* about facts. This scripture is telling us what to do with our brains. We need to regard what is positive and dwell on the good things in life, rather than what has gone wrong. This does not mean we should live in denial or become unresponsive to what is real. It means that we should grow into the maturity and likeness of Jesus, who, as He faced the cross, focused on the joy set before Him (Hebrews 12:2). What we think about and what we attach emotion to, we will believe. Those beliefs affect the electromagnetic resonance around us.

1 Corinthians 13:4-7, NKJV — *Love is patient, love is kind and is not jealous; love does not brag and is not arrogant, does not act unbecomingly; it does not seek its own, is not provoked, does not take into account a wrong suffered, does not rejoice in unrighteousness, but rejoices with the truth; bears all things, believes all things, hopes all things,* *endures all things.*

In this verse, the word, "believes," is again, the Greek word, *pisteuo*. But interestingly enough, the phrase, translated, "take into account," is the Greek word, *logizomai*. We are not to meditate on and rehearse (*logizomai*) the wrongs we have suffered, because the negative beliefs that it leads to will be put into our heart resonance, as well as have a negative impact on our physical body. This does not mean that we simply ignore abuse or deny when we hurt. Truth means we acknowledge what has happened, but we don't have to dwell on it. We can use the experience as a teachable moment, and choose to see it as an opportunity to explore our ability to forgive, receive wisdom about the incident, *and deal with it.* and apply it to future experiences. Simply put, we glean what we can that is positive, and move on. Love is a strong emotion of the heart. So accordingly, if we start with the truth and bring love into the equation, we will "believe all things" (*pisteuo*) — we will be able to create beliefs based on the marriage of truth and emotion, bringing more and more of God's blessing into our lives. *unforgiveness,*

Because negative thoughts, stress, anger and hatred are so destructive to our physical bodies as well as our life in the present and future, it is important for us to understand what the Lord is saying about belief. In our human experience, we will be hurt, and we will experience emotions the Lord uses to highlight places in our lives that need healing. However, it is what we do with that emotion that impacts us long-term. The Lord wants us to take the thoughts captive that our hurts inspire, rather than dwell on them. He wants us to apply forgiveness and repentance where necessary, and then move on with our lives, taking the wisdom of the experience with us. Belief is not a secret; it is an attitude of the heart — not used as a tool to get things, but as a testimony to the goodness of God in our lives.

JOURNAL ACTIVITY:

1. *For the next 12 hours, write down each negative thought that goes through your mind. Check to see how many judgments are there about yourself, life or other people.*
2. *Challenge 5 of those judgments to determine whether they are lies or the truth.*
3. *If you find lies, what is the truth about each particular lie?*
4. *Take inventory of your life right now. What is happening that you enjoy/want in your life and what is happening that you don't enjoy or don't want in your life?*
5. *Compare the above inventory to the negative thoughts that you have written down. How many of the negative thoughts match up to the circumstances that you don't want your life?*
6. *Belief works whether it is positive belief or negative belief. How can you change the negative thoughts to more positive ways of thinking?*

4 CHAPTER

WHO AM I?

Who am I? That's a deep question that makes us dig into the very depths of our hearts. We used to hear people exploring that concept a lot in the 60's when young people would say, "I'm going to go find myself." Remembering back, people usually laughed and had a good time mocking the individual who was off on such an ethereal search; watching as he or she tried to figure out how to go about doing that. If truth be known, a person earnestly searching for the answer to that question was looking to *individuate*.

Individuation is a normal and necessary developmental milestone in the course of human development. Much of it is accomplished during adolescence, which explains why those years can be so tumultuous! As it often turns out, how we answer the question of who we are depends on how we first answer the question, "What is Identity?"

The Bible's flagship verse concerning Identity

Proverbs 22:6 NKJV — *Train up a child in the way he should go and when he is old, he will not depart from it.*

As was said earlier, in this verse, the sense we get from the original Hebrew is that we must discern the natural bent of the child, and train up him or her to be the person God created that child to be. What this verse is really saying is that if you train up a child *in the way [of himself], and when he is old he will not depart from [who he is].* Doesn't that make a lot more sense than the notion that we should impose our own idea of who we would like our child to be? This verse pointedly defines the responsibility of parents. Parents are to see and understand their children, pay attention to them, and in a very real sense, *learn them.* Questions a parent might ask could be: "What is my child good at?" "How do they see life?" "What is their personality like?" "What kind of person are they?" "What comes naturally to them?"

Ancient Hebrews did not believe in molding a child to their own liking. They believed that every child comes into the world endowed with its own special blueprint. If a father wanted his son to be an athlete, but his son was by nature an artist, the father was expected to sacrifice his own ambitions for the boy, and so actualize God's plan for him.

Funk and Wagnall defines identity as: 1) the state

of being a specific person or thing and no other; 2) the distinctive character belonging to an individual. By simple definition, this means "value."

So what is our *primary* identity? Each individual answers this question based upon pre-existing images already established deep within them from childhood by the people who were primary in their lives. As stated in the previous chapter, parents and close authority figures are the main source of input into children's lives. They have a huge impact on how children see themselves, and how they learn to relate to the world. Children are wired to view their parents as the ultimate authority. Under a certain age, they don't consider that their parents are being untruthful, so whether the message to them is positive or negative, they will believe what they are told. God's intention is that parents should impart HIS message of identity and destiny throughout the growing years.

JOURNAL ACTIVITY:

1. *What were some of the things people told you about yourself when you were a child?*
2. *What images do you have of yourself? Based on what kind of information?*
3. *How have things people have told you about yourself affected you positively?*
4. *How have images you have of yourself affected you positively?*
5. *How have things that people have told you about yourself affected you negatively?*
6. *How have images you have of yourself affected you negatively?*

5 CHAPTER

PERSONAL IDENTITY VS. IDENTITY IN CHRIST

In the beginning of a child's life, the child has two courses to choose from: personal value or value by performance. This relates back to those two questions we discussed earlier: *"Am I loveable?"* and *"Can I trust you to meet my needs?"*

Personal value comes from parents consistently valuing their child for who the child is, rather than for good or bad behavior. Behavior comes out of either who we are or who we falsely believe we are, and we usually live up to our highest belief about ourselves. Performance, on the other hand, comes from personal value not being communicated and behavior being elevated. This often results in a false identity.

Failure to understand the difference between *who we are* and *what we do* instills within us the belief that other people have a right to determine our value. Test this theory for a minute. Would your first reaction be to say that a person like Donald Trump or Queen Elizabeth would be more valuable than say...you? And would they be more valuable than Charles Manson? If you answered yes to either of these questions, you would be wrong. Their value as human beings is determined by God — He made each of them, and He is no respecter of persons. There is, however, a fundamental difference in their behavior, in their attitudes towards life, and in their treatment of their fellow man. Their *behavior* is what others have the ability to judge as acceptable or unacceptable, and that is different than who they are as human beings.

When we fundamentally believe that other people know more about us than we can know about ourselves, we tend to take on false identities they put on us through abuse, name-calling, inaccurate prophetic words, negative predictions of a dark future ("You'll never amount to anything"), or simply wrong perceptions or judgments. Other people tell us things all the time, and although we may think we aren't listening to them, the truth of the matter is that we weigh what they say in the light of what we *know* is true about ourselves, and accept or disagree based on those assumptions.

Jesus said in Luke 6: 43-45, NKJV:

For a good tree does not bear bad fruit, nor does a bad tree bear good fruit. For every tree is known by its own fruit. For men do not gather figs from thorns, nor do they gather grapes from a bramble bush. A good man out of the good treasure of his heart brings forth good; and an evil man out of the evil treasure of his heart brings forth evil. For out of the abundance of the heart his mouth speaks.

Walking in truth about anything produces good fruit; if you are consistently producing good fruit in your life, you have good treasure in your heart. In ways in which the fruit is not so good, you are not walking in truth. It is a relatively simple equation. You know that what you believe about yourself is true if it produces good fruit consistently — you are in good emotional and physical health, your life isn't full of stress and strife, you can handle adversity when it comes your way, and your relationships are stable, to give just a few examples.

We would not be walking in truth if the fruit of our lives was not congruent with what we believed to be true of ourselves. It goes back to that old saying that if you think you are a leader and turn around to find that no one is following, you are probably just out for a walk. But our identity cannot be found in roles (such as that of a leader), jobs, ministries, callings, or gifting. If it is found in what we do, rather than who we are, at the point when those temporal facets are taken away, we can become empty and lost. Some temporal identities that can be lost are: wife/husband, mother/father, grandmother/grandfather, CEO, pastor, teacher, etc. Empty nest syndrome is all about false identities. For example, if a woman's identity is all about being a mother, when her children leave the home, her reason for being leaves as well. She is left feeling empty and without purpose. But if her belief about herself was balanced with true identity, children leaving home might then become a celebration of their maturity and a new beginning for them, even though she will miss them dearly.

JOURNAL ACTIVITY:

1. *With regard to your identity, what values did you learn from your family of origin?*
2. *Do you still believe those values are correct?*
3. *Do you tend to believe negative things about yourself that others tell you? If so, why?*

The good fruit in Jesus' life had to be people being healed, set free from demons, being fed, shown mercy, because if the good fruit was that people thought well of him - then He wouldn't have had good fruit because most leaders didn't treat Him well.

Jesus displayed love, joy, peace, goodness, kindness, gentleness, patience, faithfulness, + self-control.
He did get angry + use a whip + call some hypocrites

6 CHAPTER

LOST IDENTITY

Lost identity is the product of a skewed belief system about self. Whether it results from abuse, neglect, or subtle messages that come from our society, losing identity disconnects us from a true understanding of our Creator. It distorts the image of who God has created us to be. It keeps us from the destiny God has determined for us. It keeps us from walking in the abundance of life that comes from being who we truly are.

In the story of Adam and Eve, we can see that there are clear consequences which come from being disconnected from our Creator. This produces confusion about who we are and why we were created — or as we have said before, lack of identity. Once the fall of Adam and Eve was orchestrated, they became disoriented. They began to make decisions based on confusion — decisions which did not line up with the truth of who they were. In Genesis, Chapter Three, we see that after the fall, Adam became fearful and ashamed. He had spent his life conversing directly with God, yet he and Eve were now hiding in the bushes when God called to them. Verse seven says they were ashamed of their bodies, so they made coverings for themselves; they considered themselves less valuable/worthy because they were naked. How many of us can relate to that? If we don't look like the men and women we see on TV or on magazine covers, we experience a sense of shame. This is what porn does to women.

Adam and Eve developed feelings of insecurity. To hide their insecurity, Adam blamed Eve for his behavior, and Eve blamed the serpent for her behavior. Neither one had the confidence to be responsible for the decisions they had made. Insecurity is a symptom that accompanies a lack of identity. We become insecure about mistakes we make, considering those behaviors as making us less valuable to others.

Insecurity caused Adam to change his perception of God. Verse ten says that Adam was afraid of God, although he had never been afraid of Him before. What changed? God didn't change; it was Adam's perception of himself and how He thought God now saw him. We do the same thing. We may believe that we have done something so terrible that God has stopped loving us, or that we have disappointed Him. With that belief, we withdraw from Him. Maybe we stop praying or going to church. It is shame that causes us to believe He thinks less of us, when that is not the case at all.

We also take our eyes off the Lord and put the focus on ourselves. When Adam and Eve became aware of their nakedness, the need to cover up shame became their focus. Then, rather than asking God for clothing, they created their own. They chose to rely on themselves instead of God.

Lessons From an Old Friend

Several years ago, I took my precious 22-year-old cat to the vet and had her put to sleep. Over the previous six years, she and I had fought a well-waged war against kidney disease. We walked a very fine line between health and sickness, until one day, she couldn't do it anymore. In the time I cared for her, I grew to understand her very intimately. For example, there were several different sounds she made, depending on how she was feeling. There was a specific look that came across her face when she wanted to be left alone. And when she needed comfort, she would climb up on my right shoulder and just lie there until I had to put her down.

There were many lessons I learned from her over the years, many having to do with unconditional love. I learned that an animal's love is probably the closest example God gave us on this earth of unconditional love. She always loved me, no matter what. Even as I made the decision to end her life, she continued to teach me about the selflessness it takes to put another life before your own. I understood that after 22 years I would no longer have that little calico ball of fur sleeping on the end of my bed, or be able to reach over and scratch her ear as she lay on the sofa next to me. I wouldn't hear her purr like a freight train in the middle of the night or wake up to her waiting patiently by my side to notice that it was time for breakfast! All of these are precious memories for me, but even in her death, she taught me one more valuable lesson.

That morning, rather than putting her in her carrier, I took her fluffy pink blanket and laid it on the seat next to me in the car. She laid quietly on the blanket as we made the short fifteen minute drive to the veterinarian's office. Along the way, I talked to her about how special she was and how much I would miss her. She listened quietly, as if she knew exactly what I was saying. I had been through this process quite a few times with other animals, so I knew what to expect, but the stark realization is never easy.

The veterinarian and his staff were very comforting as we entered into the very difficult and heart-wrenching process. Once everything was done and it was clear that she was gone, the staff left me alone in the room with her to say my goodbyes. It was then that she taught me the last lesson I would be privileged to learn from her. It was a quiet realization as I sat there, gazing at her laying on the countertop. I began to realize that the body I was seeing held no connection for me. I thought that was odd, but the more I felt it, the more I understood that the part of her I had always been connected to was no longer there. It wasn't her physical body that I loved; it was the part of her that was inside that made her eyes twinkle, that caused her to play with her favorite string, and that gave her life. As that realization settled in, I was able to get up, leave the room and drive quietly home.

In the days after her death, I thought a lot about what I had learned. I remember as a young girl how important I thought it was to look just right, have my hair just the right way, wear "cool" clothes, and do all the things that we think makes us attractive to the opposite sex. As I thought about that, I realized that the most real connections we make with people are like the connection I had with my cat. That connection is not based on outward appearance; it is based on who others are on the inside. Whatever you want to call it — heart, spirit, personality, etc., what we connect with in another person is not on the outside. It develops from an intimate connection with who they are on the inside — the part that truly makes them who they are. When you connect with a family member, friend or spouse in such a deep way, a strong bond is built, and the outward appearance often becomes unimportant.

So many people believe that if we are drawn to the outward appearance that's all that matters. Young, hot and sexy is all that seems to be valued in our society. Couples who use that as a foundation for their relationship often find that it is like building your house on sand, and that it falls apart after a period of time. Scripture teaches us that man looks on the outward appearance, but God looks on the heart (1 Samuel 16:17). The lesson I learned from my cat was the truth of that Scripture: who we are is on the inside, not the outside. It has to do with character and love and joy and integrity. Who we are on the inside is what will leave this mortal body and live on into eternity.

When we are unable to connect with the spirit of another because we have accepted the lie that says we have to *look* good, we end up feeling rejected, inferior, and not good enough. The wounds of our soul cover up who we really *are* on the inside, making it difficult for others to connect with us in a fulfilling way.

If we truly understand this lesson, it might cause us to stop spending so much money, time, and effort to improve what we look like on the outside, and spend our time improving who we are on the inside. It is really not about what we look like or how talented we are; it is about *who* we are!

If we can come to the place where we see as Jesus sees, we will begin to value our friends and loved ones, and connect on a heart level. It is only then that we will be color blind, not status-oriented, and unconcerned about the current fashion trend. We will be able to love our neighbor as ourselves and fulfill the greatest commandment Jesus gave us.

JOURNAL ACTIVITY:

1. *If you are married, why do you love your spouse?*
2. *What are the qualities you value about your best friend?*
3. *What do you appreciate about your child/children?*

7 CHAPTER

A PROFILE OF LOST IDENTITY

A general profile for a person who lacks identity usually looks something like this:

1. The person will usually try to please everyone, and in some cases, overly agree with what others say, trying to be what others want them to be or what they perceive to be acceptable to others.

2. If they have an opinion, they may or may not express it, but if they do express it and others disagree, they may retract their

statement or doubt that their opinion is right.

3. They may not be able to make decisions or uphold their decisions in the face of a stronger personality.

4. They often can't identify what they feel, and may be limited to just a few feelings that are socially permitted. For example, in our society, anger is more commonly acceptable for men than for women. Tears are more commonly acceptable for women than for men.

5. Often they find their identity in things, roles, or possessions; when these are removed, they become confused, disoriented and depressed.

6. They don't know what their purpose is or what their destiny may be. They often have felt unfulfilled in their career, and may change careers frequently.

7. Once they learn the game, they may not want to deviate from the rules; they often have difficulty with change.

8. Conflict becomes an issue for persons who aren't sure of who they are, so they tend to avoid it. These individuals usually come from homes where conflict was never resolved. Children who grow up witnessing unresolved conflicts learn that it never ends, or that it ends badly. So, internally, they make decisions not to engage in it.

9. When abuse is involved…

a. These individuals often fail to realize that being treated rudely or abusively is not acceptable.

b. They don't consider the fact that they have choices and have the power to remove themselves from these situations.

c. They don't realize that their opinions count just as much as others' do.

d. Parents who grew up in abusive conditions may sacrifice themselves for their children rather than making the decision to remove themselves and their children from the offender.

10. It is common to see an individual who feels like an imposter in life.

a. They avoid being vulnerable, lest they be "found out."

b. They may be tremendously gifted and talented, but believe that if someone "better" comes along they can be replaced.

11. Lack of identity also produces a wandering through life.

a. Because they don't understand who they are, or exactly what makes up the person they're supposed to be, they compare themselves to other people. Thus, they fail to find their way into their true destiny.

b. If they see other people being blessed, they may try to make that blessing work for them. "A friend of mine made a lot of money doing that, I think I'll give it a try." It is as though they keep putting on *other people's coats,* trying to make them fit or look good on themselves.

The fruit of having little or no identity will differ from person to person according to temperament and personal choices. The following comprises a partial list of possibilities:

1. They don't know what to think or feel.
2. They need someone else to tell them who they are and that they are OK.
3. They change to fit expectations, demands, or circumstances — they become a chameleon.
4. They lack self-confidence.
5. They may put themselves down, or they may seem over-confident, and bluff a lot.
6. They are often co-dependent, not knowing where others end and they begin.
7. They have to work or perform to earn love, value and acceptance.
8. They may often be tired, and may burn out (because of having to perform).
9. They may be self-sacrificing in an unhealthy way; they may become a "martyr."

10. They are easily controlled.
11. They are often victims with very few, if any, healthy boundaries.
12. They may not be able to engage or connect with people, or allow others to connect with them.
13. They often cannot accept gifts or compliments without reciprocating; they may not be able to accept gifts or compliments at all.
14. They may be jealous of others, and often feel displaced.
15. They have a lot of shame.
16. They often struggle with addictions to numb the shame.
17. They may wear a lot of masks.

How do you know what true identity is? Simply put, identity is comprised of individual qualities that will not change. That does not include items like being over or under-weight, political views or, sometimes, even religious views. Those can change with knowledge and maturity. The things that make you unique stay constant over time. Like whether you are tall, short, blue-eyed, of German descent or Italian. Whether you are musically inclined or not, are an animal lover, have a gift for the sciences, are artistic, are more compassionate or tend to be analytical. In your heart of hearts, do you enjoy nature, gardening, seed planting, etc., or are you more inclined toward working on cars and being mechanically gifted? If you are energized by having time alone to read or paint or cook, you probably will not be found delighting in crowds of people or having an overly active social life. These are qualities that don't change. But even changeable preferences may give clues as to the person you are. If you absolutely hated tomatoes as a kid, but relish them now, could it be that you are a naturally flexible person? If your favorite color is purple, you may not like wearing orange clothing. If your favorite color to wear is purple one week and orange the next, could it be that you have a heart that loves variety as the spice of life? These are traits that don't change.

It is important to know these things about yourself, or you may find yourself engaging in activities or careers that don't suit you very well. God has built into each of us certain ways that we drink in life, and if we don't know what those are, or choose not to engage in them for one reason or another, we tend to get depressed and burned out.

JOURNAL ACTIVITY:

1. *Have you seen any evidence of lack of identity in your family or in people you work with?* Yes, my Mom

2. *Where in your own life are you able to see distortions of who you are?*

3. *How has a distorted self-image produced loss of identity in you?*

4. *What positive things has God (or others) told you about yourself that you can't believe?*

8 CHAPTER

CLOSE ENCOUNTERS

If we have gotten lost, how do we begin the journey toward regaining our identity? One of the first things we have to do is listen to God and believe what He says about us. Often that means listening to those things in our hearts that we have been denying, because the Lord does speak to our hearts. Psalm 37:4 says, *God...will give you the desires of your heart.* This doesn't mean that He always gives us what we desire; it does mean that He puts desires there. If God has put a desire in your heart, you will want to pay attention to it. That desire is a clue to your identity and your purpose in life.

Here are four examples from the Bible of people who had an encounter with God and either discovered who they were or went on believing lies in their hearts about themselves.

SAUL

Read 1 Samuel 9:3-10

Saul came from the lineage of a very powerful man in the tribe of Benjamin. Saul was very handsome and somewhat imposing due to his stature. He was sent out with his servant to find some lost donkeys. It is interesting to note that when Saul despaired of finding the donkeys and decided to go back home, the servant disagreed. Saul's response was not that of a confident man; his answer was rather whiney. He gave excuses for why they shouldn't go on, which his servant countered with a solution — he persuaded Saul to enquire of the prophet Samuel.

Read 1 Samuel 9:19-21

Although it was customary to come in humility when enquiring of the Lord through a man of God, you might expect a different kind of tone than Saul's. Samuel gave him the information he needed about the lost donkeys, but in the process there is an interesting response from Saul in verse 21. Saul points out that he comes from a very insignificant family in one of the smallest tribes of Israel. Isn't that quite a contradiction to what was said about him in verse one of the same chapter? The author of 1 Samuel describes Saul's father as a mighty man of power. Perhaps there was an error in Saul's perception of himself and his family.

Read 1 Samuel 10:5-9

When Saul met Samuel, Samuel told Saul who he was several times; speaking out Saul's true identity. He treated Saul with honor and respect, blessed him and anointed him King over Israel. In verse six, he told Saul that the Lord was going to enable him to prophesy, and that he would be turned into another man. In verse nine, Saul, having had a personal encounter with God, received a new heart.

Read 1 Samuel 10: 10-16

Here, Saul prophesied alongside the prophets. He has been changed in such a way that people who knew him before this encounter are commenting that he was among the prophets and were astonished. His uncle met him and began to ask him about his journey. It is very interesting to note that while Saul told him about the donkeys and meeting Samuel, he neglected to tell him that he had been anointed King of Israel!

Read 1 Samuel 10: 17-24

Saul was called up before the people to officially receive recognition and be installed in his office as king. If this was you or me, don't you think we would be pretty excited? Don't you think we would consider this to be such a high honor that we would be at least *available* for the coronation? But where do we find Saul? …Hiding among the baggage, and someone had to be sent away from the festivities to find him and bring him to Samuel so that he could be recognized.

After reading this story, we find that all the things

God did for Saul and enabled him to do, did not
change the fundamental insecurity and lack of
confidence in Saul's heart. Saul's purpose and
destiny was to become Israel's first king, yet the lie
that Saul held in his heart, the lie that we see
infecting his belief about himself as a young man,
continued to plague him throughout his reign. When
David arrived on the scene, Saul saw him as a threat,
and that perceived threat drove him mad. In truth,
David was not a threat to Saul. Saul's insecurities
and resulting behaviors made him unstable; but even
then, God did not remove him from the throne. Saul
ended his own life, a tortured and angry man. The
treasure in his heart was not good, and drove him to
a bad end.

JACOB

Read Genesis 27:1-29

Jacob's parents, Rebekah and Isaac, were very
disconnected. They were the kind of parents who
dwelt more on the behavior of their children than on
who they were as people. In Genesis 27, you see that
Isaac was going to bless Esau, but instead of just
blessing him, he requested that Esau do something to
earn that blessing — he asked Esau to go hunting
and then use the meat to make him his favorite stew.
When that was done, he would bless him. The
message Isaac sent (which was probably not the first
time), was that you have to earn your love, as well as
your blessing.

Jacob's mother, Rebekah, was so disconnected at

the heart level that she sold out one son over the other. When Rebecca heard that Isaac was going to bless Esau, she put a plan into place to steal Esau's birthright, and give it to her favorite. What kind of mother does a thing like that? But then again, what parents would give their child a name that meant "deceiver/usurper"? These are some very disconnected people! As a result of their dysfunction, these two brothers probably had issues with each other; once the blessing was stolen, they most certainly did. This was the ultimate "Mom liked you best" story!

Isaac was just as off balance as his wife. Even though he was blind, wouldn't you think that if he had a close relationship with his sons, he would have known one from the other? Think about it; if you are a parent, even with your eyes closed, wouldn't you be able to tell which of your children you were talking to? Would there not be some clue....the sound of their voice, the smell of their hair, the sound of their footsteps as they walked toward you? Isaac could not tell the difference between his eldest son and his youngest son; what does that say about his relationship with them?

We see a set of parents who are not in unity with each other and a father who does not know his sons. Do you think there may have been some problems in that home?

Read Genesis 27:30-41
In verse 34, we read: *When Esau heard the words of his father, he cried with an exceedingly great and*

bitter cry, and said to his father, "Bless me – me also, O my father!"

Look at the descriptive words here - *exceedingly great and bitter cry.* This young man was heartbroken; he was hurt to the very core of his being. His blessing had been stolen from him. The blessing was very tangibly real and important in Hebrew culture; it was more than just words of support — it was a literal power from on high. Esau *knew* that without it, his life could not prosper. He had lost some very valuable things. He had lost the blessing and he had already lost his inheritance when he sold it to Jacob for a bowl of lentil stew. Interestingly enough, he did not grieve for that loss as he did for his blessing. Although Isaac later gave Esau a blessing of his own, it did not satisfy him as much as the one he lost, even though Isaac foretold his eventual ability to become his own man and rise up in his own identity.

The Holy Spirit is our blessing

Read Genesis 27:42-45

Rebekah saw the strife she had created between the two brothers. She advised Jacob to go away for a short time until Esau would forget what had been done to him, and then everything would be alright. Again, we see the level of disconnect in Rebekah. Esau wanted to *KILL* Jacob! Is it even within the realm of possibility that Esau would simply *"forget"* what had happened, and *his fury will turn away?* She didn't seem to have a good grasp on the intensity of feeling she had created here — the depth of the pain one of her sons was in. She minimized the situation in order to resolve the problem. This is a pattern we find often in dysfunctional homes, where no one takes responsibility for their actions. There are underlying problems; there is a lack of empathy for one another, and then when things blow apart, everyone runs to their separate corners until it blows over.

Read Genesis 27:46-32:21

Jacob went to stay with his uncle Laban, and seemed to be prompted by lies of his own. He lies to and deceives this family as well, to the extent that in chapter 31, Laban could no longer trust him. He made Laban so angry that, to avoid his wrath, he ended up sneaking away with his wives and flocks in the middle of the night. This had to be difficult for Jacob, as he now had both sides of the family angry at him, and for good reason! The consequences of his name's meaning had come back to haunt him, and he must have felt very frightened. However, the Lord had mercy on Jacob and encouraged him that He would be with him. Although this may have had a profound effect on Jacob, it didn't resolve the issue with his brother Esau that still loomed before him. By the time we get to Chapter 32, verse 22, we find Jacob in desperate straits.

Read Genesis 32:22-30

At this point, we find Jacob desperate. He knew his brother was coming. He was fully aware of what he had done to him, and he didn't know what kind of a greeting he was going to get. He could only imagine that his brother was still angry and was coming to do him harm, if not kill him.

However, again the Lord stepped in and made a change in Jacob's heart that he needed in order to move forward. Jacob wrestled with God, but instead of reacting angrily, God spoke healing to Jacob's heart. He took away the name, Jacob ("deceiver/usurper"), which was only a reflection of his behavior. In its place he bestowed a new name, Israel, which means, "fights with God," and signifies that he was an over-comer. The bad fruit that had been in his heart — the lies that did not line up with who God created him to be, were removed. From that time on, we see a different Jacob. Jacob now understood who he was, because God had identified the good qualities within him and blessed them. That changed his life. By the time he met his brother Esau, he had become a humble man.

Read Genesis 32:22-30

Changes continue throughout Jacob's life as the story continues to unfold, until, in Genesis 49, we see Jacob blessing his twelve sons. Jacob did not bless his sons in the same way that Isaac had blessed him. Isaac's blessing was merely a description of what Jacob would do, what would happen to him, and how people would treat him....but when Jacob blessed his sons, he told them *WHO THEY WERE*. When he blessed his sons, he became the sensitive molder of destinies that God had originally designed him to be.

   a. Genesis 49:9a, 10a, NKJV: *You are a lion's cub, O Judah...The scepter will not depart from Judah, nor the ruler's staff from between his feet.*

   b. Genesis 16a, 17, NKJV: *.Dan will provide justice for his people...Dan will be a serpent by the roadside, a viper along the path, that bites the horse's heels so that its rider tumbles backward.*

   c. V 21, NKJV: *Naphtali is a doe set free that bears beautiful fawns.*

There is a vast difference between the blessing Isaac gave Jacob and the blessings Jacob gave his sons, and this is a testament to the restoration of a life that had gone very wrong — a tribute to the power of how identity can change a persons' direction, put him on the right path, and cause him to flourish. Because Jacob had an encounter with God Who told him who HE was, Jacob truly learned to see the hearts of his sons.

His twelve sons would go on to spawn a dozen tribes — with an identity that would transform the world and usher in the Messiah!

GIDEON

Read Judges 6:11-23

In this story, we find Gideon threshing wheat in a wine press, hidden from view so the Midianites would not find the grain. An angel of the Lord appeared and said, "The Lord is with you, you mighty man of valor" (vs. 12). Again, we find a discrepancy between how the Lord sees someone and in what he believes about himself. If Gideon had truly believed he was a "mighty man of valor," he might not have hidden in a wine press, nor protested to the angel about his people's situation. The details of his protest revealed that he believed God hadn't done anything for Israel, had abandoned them and himself, as he was a part of Israel. He believed that he was of little stature or consequence. *I am the least* (vs. 15). Furthermore, he asked for proof that an angel would really talk to him, requesting that the angel cause fire to flare from a rock and cook a meal he prepared (vs. 17-22). Gideon doubted himself, and he doubted God. He is the type of individual we discussed earlier, who doesn't believe in himself and doesn't trust other people.

Mercifully, the angel proved himself to this doubting man, and Gideon understood his worth. Gideon accepted that his belief about himself was in error, and he chose to believe what the Angel had said about him. In verse 22, we find Gideon admitting how imperceptive he had been about the angel's identity, and we hear the blessing of the Lord as he quieted Gideon's heart and assured him of his safety.

Once Gideon accepted the truth about himself, and understood who he was and what he was called to do, he was able to step into his destiny and become the mighty man of valor that the Lord had created him to be. He destroyed the altar of Baal and went on to subdue the Midianites with 300 men!

PAUL

Read Acts 9:1-22

Saul considered it his job to murder Christians. He made plans to kill some of them, round up the rest, and bring them back to Jerusalem for trial. Paul was a passionate man, intelligent and scholarly. He was determined to right the wrongs that he saw in society, and had the power and influence to do so. He had no reservations that what he was doing was wrong. His driven, type-A personality propelled him into a direct encounter with the God who had created him.

Although Saul believed it was his job to eradicate Jesus' followers, from the beginning of time he had been selected as a *chosen vessel of Mine to bear My name before gentiles, kings and the children of Israel* (vs. 9). How can a man with this kind of destiny have gotten it so wrong?

This day on the Damascus road, Jesus Himself confronted Paul with love and truth, and it broke through the hardness of his heart. He came to understand his true purpose, and with that understanding Saul (who would become "Paul" in Chapter Thirteen) shifted into his identity and was propelled into history as a crusader for Christ to the Gentiles and a planter of churches throughout the Roman Empire. He is thought to have been the one (rather than Matthias), who should have replaced Judas Iscariot after his betrayal of Jesus and ultimate suicide. Paul is credited as the author of a major portion of the New Testament.

Summary

What we see in all these stories is a consistent theme — all these men did not know who they were, and therefore, were not receiving the full blessing of God in their lives. They were not living the lives that God had intended for them to live. They needed to shake loose the false identities they had accepted. Once they accepted the truth about themselves, they were able to move forward into their destinies with power, anointing, and blessing.

The truth about who we are, and our acceptance of that truth, looses the provision and blessing of God that propels us forward into the life He has created for us. We can be like King Saul, accepting our promotion, but then spending our lives in strife, never believing that we are good enough for the position into which we have been placed. Or we can be like Jacob, who spent many years stealing from others in order to get what he thought he was entitled to. Like Gideon, we can spend our lives in fear and hiding, believing we aren't good enough or blessed enough to live a life of victory. Or like Paul, we may be on a path that has nothing to do with who we are, and must be knocked on our behinds and rendered helpless in order to see the light. Sound familiar? In any case, the bottom line is that we need to know the truth and the truth will set us free, as it did for Jacob, Gideon and Paul. Unwrapping true identity always involves recognizing and dealing with foundational lies we have believed about ourselves.

JOURNAL ACTIVITY:

1. *Which of the four men do you most identify with? Why?*
2. *What lies or limiting beliefs do you see in your own life?*
3. *What is the truth that you will put in place of those lies?*

9 CHAPTER

HOW ARE YOU GIFTED?

Another part of the puzzle of who we are has to do with our gifts and talents. According to scripture, there are three categories of gifts:

The manifestation gifts, found in 1 Corinthians 12:7-10

- Word of Wisdom
- Word of Knowledge
- Faith
- Healing
- Miracles
- Distinguishing Between Types of Spirits
- Tongues

• Interpretation of Tongues

The ministry gifts are found in Ephesians 4:8

• Apostle
• Prophet
• Evangelist
• Pastor
• Teacher

The motivational gifts are found in Romans 12:6-8

• Prophesying/perceiving
• Serving
• Teaching
• Exhorting
• Giving
• Administration
• Showing mercy/compassion

Now admittedly, the subject of gifts is one that raises a lot of questions and discussion in the body of Christ. These discussions are beyond the scope of this writing. However, I will comment on the motivational gifts. These are the gifts that motivate us in life. We tend to view life through one or more of these perspectives, and if we have characteristics that fall in line with the characteristics of one or more of these gifts, that will give us more clues as to who we are and how we are made. These gifts tend to give us clues about our natural skill sets and how we see life in general.

To find out what motivates us, we may want to engage in some research. Although many of us don't have the kinds of direct encounters with the Lord we have described, God does give us a fundamental sense of who we are, and provides moments of decision along the way that have the effect of uncovering truth and adjusting our course. There may be truths we once knew about ourselves that have gotten buried or forgotten. But we can start developing a strong sense of those truths through events that challenge our value systems and bring us to a place where we have to define what we can live with and what we can't. Often, our search leads us to receive acknowledgement of personality traits through family members, or through personality and career tests. This can give us permission to trust what we know deep inside to be true to ourselves. No matter what strategy God uses, He is always in the business of putting truth before us and waiting for us to accept it.

We may also need to remember who we were in our earliest life. Memories will give us clues. What gave us joy? What were our interests? What were our best subjects in school? What did people consistently observe about us? As we remember these things, we can translate them into the present day, and reflect on how we see ourselves now. What, if any, of these things still ring true today?

If, as a child, you very much enjoyed animals and had dogs or cats, perhaps one thing you can do to bring more joy into your life is to get a pet, or volunteer some time at your local humane society, walking the dogs or caring for and playing with the cats. If you loved to take things apart and discover what made them tick, maybe you have the ability to build or repair things. I remember a friend of mine saying that his dad used to love to play in the dirt when he was a kid. He would build roads and hills, and then drive his toy cars around what he had built. Guess what he chose as a career field? He started his own construction business. He builds roads, breaks ground on new housing developments, digs basements, etc. He owns tractors and graders and big trucks, and still loves to play in the dirt, only now he does it for a living! To help discover your specific preferences, I have included a checklist in the appendix that may act like an interview to help you decide.

We can also seek out assessments designed to help us understand our temperament, see what motivates us, identify what our passions and interests are, and help us decide what we truly believe, and why. These types of assessments can be given by any career counselor, and usually don't cost a lot of money. Check to see if your local college has a career counseling office, and make an appointment with one of the counselors.

Another thing we can do is to invest in some counseling, which can help us expose the roots of why we put value on what we do rather than who we are. In doing that, we should look for:

• Shame
• Neglect

• Lack of blessing
• Broken trust
• Decisions to abandon who we are

Additionally, we need to understand the difference between our personal identity and our identity in Christ. Previously, we discussed this, but as a reminder, identity in Christ is a positional identity. It describes what Jesus has done for us and *every* other person in the body of Christ. Personal identity is how the Lord uniquely created us as *individuals* for our unique place in this world. Therefore, praying with the understanding that He wants to show us who we are and how He created us is vital to the journey. The Lord is on our side as we approach this task, and He will provide the opportunities, the open doors, and the revelations which will reveal the truth.

With regard to having a place in this world, here are some examples of historical figures that were placed specifically in time, with unique gifts, to be able to carry out an observable plan:

• **John the Baptist:** he was the forerunner of Jesus Christ, and proclaimed Him as the Messiah. John faced a tremendous amount of adversity and ridicule as he carried out the task he knew he was created to do.
• **Abraham Lincoln:** he was President of the U.S. during the Civil War, and was responsible for ending the tradition of slavery in this country.
• **Alexander Fleming:** he discovered penicillin in

1928.

- **Franklin D. Roosevelt:** he was President of the U.S. during the great depression and most of the Second World War.
- **David Ben-Gurion:** he was vital in the creation of the state of Israel, and was Israel's first prime minister.
- **Rosa Parks:** she is credited by the U.S. Congress as being the "mother of the modern day civil rights movement."
- **John F Kennedy:** he was President of the U.S. during the Cuban missile crisis when weapons capable of attacking the mainland were positioned 90 miles from the coast.
- **The books of the Bible** were assembled by a world-wide convocation of bishops at the Councils of Laodicea (about A.D. 363) and Carthage (A.D. 397).

What these individuals were able to do came out of who they were. They weren't perfect, but they were individuals who knew who they were and what they stood for. Because of that, they had the ability and grace to stand for what they believed, develop a plan, and carry it out. They were uniquely qualified for the destinies they were designed to live.

Allow God to Show You Your Family Blessing.

Gen 12:2-3, NKJV: *I will make you a great nation; I will bless you and make your name great; and you shall be a blessing. I will bless those who bless you* *and I will curse him who curses you; and in you all the families of the earth shall be blessed.*

I have a friend whose husband came to see me for a counseling session. He is of Asian descent. Unfortunately, when he would go for ministry, he found it common that counselors would look for generational blockages that might account for some of the issues he and his family were experiencing in present day life.

We talked for a little while at the beginning of the session, and he began telling me a little about his family history — many hundreds of years had been documented on both sides of his family. He mentioned that his ancestors had been physicians in the courts of one of the emperors. As we discussed family matters, he mentioned that he was very proud of his son. I asked him why, and he said that it gave him such joy to see him derive so much happiness out of praying for people. His son had a great desire to see people healed of illnesses. He related that a few days before, he had watched his son pray for a lady, and he had admired the faith and passion he had witnessed.

It was at that moment that it clicked for me — hundreds of years after his family had been physicians in the emperor's court, there was still a calling on his family for healing! The power of the Lord fell upon us, and he began to thank the Lord for the gift that his family had been given. He repented for any people in his family who had abandoned their identity and the calling on their lives. Things changed for him in those few minutes that day. He had an encounter with the Lord that showed him who he was, and the blessing that was still on his family. Since then, I have heard of miraculous things that have happened to that family, successes they have experienced, and victories that have come their way, simply because he accepted the truth about who he was. He didn't have to apologize to me, to God, or anyone else about there being individuals in his family line who weren't Christians. He stood in the truth of the blessing of God, and that changed things for him.

2 Timothy 1:5-6, NKJV: *when I call to remembrance the genuine faith that is in you, which dwelt first in your grandmother Lois, and your mother Eunice, and I am persuaded is in you also. Therefore I remind you to stir up the gift of God which is in you..."*

When a parent looks into a child's eyes and tells that child who he or she is, changes reverberate throughout the world and the generations to come. When we see people with God's eyes —see who they truly are and validate that truth, identities of nations might very well become our inheritance!

According to the American Heritage Dictionary, the word, "VALIDATE," means: "to mark with an indication of official sanction; to establish the soundness of; corroborate."

JOURNAL ACTIVITY:

1. *Can you think of any more individuals like those listed previously who were strategically placed in history to be able to deal with defining moments in our world's timeline?*
2. *In the movie, "It's a Wonderful Life," George Bailey wishes he had never been born. When he gets his wish, he finds out that the life of everyone around him has turned out much for the worse, until he asks to have the wish reversed. Imagine: What would your family, your church and your town be like if you hadn't been born? How have you impacted life around you, just because you exist? (If you are able to, watch the movie before answering this question.)*

My mom said my grandfather (her Dad)
robbed from the rich to give to the poor.
I don't know anyone from my family
who knows our family history.
Gracie had a heart for the under dog.

10 CHAPTER

WHAT IS MY PURPOSE?

Once we answer the question, "Who am I?" with accuracy, we have a good indication of what our purpose may be and what our focus in life may be as well. Purpose has everything to do with identity. God would not gift someone with a talent to communicate and then give them a purpose that has nothing to do with communication. Can you see how that follows? Our gifts, our talents, our likes and dislikes, have everything to do with what we have been created for. It stands to reason why God's people would be challenged on this ground. If we are confused about our identity and purpose, we will also be disconnected from the resources and blessing God gives to enable us to achieve our purpose.

Doesn't that make more sense when we look at people who are struggling with their lives? It fits better with the character of God than believing that they don't have identity and destiny because they don't have enough faith, or that God simply doesn't value them enough to help them out of their struggles.

If we know the truth about who we are, then we can step into our purpose with confidence and freedom. It's all about focusing on what we were created to do, and being what we were created to be, and trusting that His blessings will follow. The abundant life, the anointing, the blessings — all follow the truth. The truth is in our original blueprint, not the facade we have created. We have seen this in Jacob, Gideon and Paul. These men accepted their true identities, and the anointing of God propelled them forward. They didn't have to think about provision; they didn't have to develop a marketing plan. They simply changed course, and God provided the rest.

Now to be clear, this does not mean we won't ever struggle in life; we will. Paul did. Jesus did. We can't expect to be any different. However, if we face our struggles from a position of strength, which identity gives us, we can endure. We can finish the race. We can fight the good fight.

Several portions of scripture illustrate this point. In 1 Kings 17:1, Elijah prophesied to King Ahab that the people were to expect a drought. This drought was coming because of King Ahab's sins. To preserve Elijah, God instructed him to leave the area and go hide by the Brook Cherith, and He directed ravens to deliver food to him there. If Elijah had decided sit down by the road a few miles before he arrived at the brook, and create a nice little hammock with an umbrella to keep out the sun, the ravens would still have delivered the provision God promised to the place God intended, and Elijah would have gotten very hungry!

In Matthew 6:25-34, Jesus talked about the lilies of the field and the birds of the air. God knows them and provides for them because He created them. We often see in that passage a lesson about not worrying about the things of life because God will provide them. That is a valid truth. However, it often doesn't occur to us that this passage also affirms that creatures and plants don't pretend to be something other than what they are. A lily doesn't have to try to be a lily; it simply is a lily. The same is true of birds. A sparrow doesn't try to be an eagle; it is content with being what is was created to be, and it knows that provision will always be there. In the same way, God created us, and He knows that we need all these things.

Human beings are the only creations with the capacity to mentally separate themselves from who they truly are and see themselves as something else. So, does the scripture in Matthew six also illustrate that if we are not being true to our design, the blessing will not be on what we have created or who we think we need to be? Will it still be on what God created — our true and authentic selves? If we abandon who we are, are we walking away from the blessing? At this point in this book, with what we now know to be true, it is safe to believe that this is more than likely a true assumption.

So how does this apply to real life, you ask? The Lord may be saying to you that if you will concentrate on what your purpose is and what your passion is, and just do that, He will provide the rest.

How often, over the course of our lives, have we been preoccupied with trying to make lives and careers work, instead of just being who we are and letting life progress from there? As we have majored on the mechanics of life, doesn't it seem that what gets put off to the side is the work itself, the purpose for which we have been put here? This does not mean that we should just bumble through life, neglecting to follow the practical and true principles we have been taught. It does mean that we understand that form follows life, that ministry, career, and purpose flow out of who we truly are, not who we think we are. Additionally, the principle of giving out of what we have been given means that we can't give what we don't have. This makes it even more important to understand who we are and what we have been endowed with before we can move forward.

Luke 6:38 says: *Give, and it will be given to you: good measure, pressed down, shaken together, and running over will be put into your bosom. For with the same measure that you use, it will be measured back to you.* What is sometimes hard to grasp is that this principle doesn't just speak about money. As human beings living in a materialistic culture, we

...freely you've received— freely give...

have learned that life gravitates around money. If you don't have money, you aren't successful, you can't provide for your family, you won't be able to have the things in life that you want, and, most importantly, you won't be able to secure the basic necessities. Therefore, it is hard not to be preoccupied with the idea that having money is the goal of life. Honestly, God isn't against us having money. He knows we need it. But what grieves Him is that we often sell our souls to get it. This can be seen in an example from my own life.

When I was much younger, there was a time when a "new" kind of business was conceived of. It was known as "multi-level marketing." It was described as a way to be in business for yourself, build income, and help other people. It depended on you and how hard you wanted to work. As a prospect, you were told you could achieve anything you wanted if you just worked hard enough. Many people, including myself, dove headfirst into this concept. We paid the fees and learned the skills. We happily went out to try to convince our friends that they should do what we were doing too. Some people did really well, but others like me did not. After trying three or four different companies over a period of about ten years, watching some succeed and some miserably crash and burn, I decided that MLM wasn't for me. Well, guess what? I was right!

As I matured and healed and became more aware of who I was as a person, what brought me life and what brought me death, it turned out that I was not cut out for sales. Sales as a career, is about as far away from who I am and what my talents are as light is from dark. So it wouldn't matter what kind of MLM structure I built. It would be an empty shell, because I had very little from which I could draw to make it grow. Now that doesn't mean I don't have a deep respect for people who are gifted with the ability to sell things. In fact, if I were to ever decide that MLM or retail was something I wanted to take on, I would want a whole bunch of those people working for me! But the key is, I would have them manage the business, leaving me to do tasks more in line with my gifting and skill set. Interestingly enough, I recently took a career-interest test, just for the fun of it. It said in no uncertain terms that selling was one of the three careers I should never engage in! I had to just sit back and giggle; because that validated the very thing I knew to be true about myself.

What would have happened if I had continued to bark up that tree, and tried to grab the brass ring that so many people said was possible to obtain? I would have become mediocre at it at best, and in the end, I would have ignored a most precious commodity — the person I was created to be. I would have settled for what someone else defined as success. Much worse, I would have seen myself without value and thrown away my self-esteem because I couldn't achieve what someone else said was within my reach.

Everybody is a genius. But, if you judge a fish by its ability to climb a tree, it will spend its whole life believing that it is stupid. ~Albert Einstein

JOURNAL ACTIVITY:

1. Thinking back to childhood, what gave you joy? What were you passionate about?
2. What kinds of things give you life?
3. What kinds of things drain life from you?

11 CHAPTER

SO NOW WHAT DO I DO?

Now that you have read all of this, what will you do with it? I wish it were as easy as a simple one-size-fits-all step-by-step plan. Finding identity requires a plan of self-discovery as unique as you are. God knows your heart. He knows the hurts, the wounds and the lies that have gotten you off track. And He knows the path that will restore you to truth.

In the appendix, I have furnished you with a self-interview that will help you begin the process. As you answer the questions, don't give answers you *think* are correct; give answers you truly *feel* and *believe in your heart*. You need to understand what *your* value system is, what *your* gifts and talents are and what *your* preferences are about life. It's OK if they differ from someone else's. Once you have this information, you can begin to make decisions based on the truth, as reflected by these answers which are more in line with who *you* are. Then your task going forward is to be ***REAL***.

Give honest answers to questions that are asked of you. State your opinions with confidence because you know why you believe what you believe. You may even go as far as to change careers because you now know why the career you presently have has become unsatisfying.

Relationships are places that you may see the most movement as you become more real about yourself and your life. Try not to be concerned if people move out of your life. It is a natural consequence when you take down the façade and function as the real person you were made to be. People may be in your life because they are attracted to the façade. You may have observed that it is hard to have relationship with these people because you are often trying to keep them happy, changing things about yourself that they don't like or approve of. If they move out of your life, it simply means that they were not supposed to be there in the first place because they are attracted to individuals that look like your facade. When you become the real you, it becomes apparent that the people who move into your life or stay in your life are there because they want to be, because there is something about the real you they like to be around. These are the folks you

5·23·20

don't have to perform for or adapt to. You don't have to try so hard to maintain yourself in the relationship. In effect, you become like the lily of the field....you just are who you were created to be. Like the lily, which attracts individuals to it because they like lilies, you attract people into your life who are there because they like you. Isn't that a much better way to live?

APPENDIX

IDENTITY CHECKLIST

So many times when we lack identity, we are unable to identify that which makes us unique—our own personal strengths, spiritual gifts, preferences and opinions. As you ponder the following questions, answer them with the understanding that there is no right or wrong answer. Your answers are not going to be evaluated or judged. They are for you — to help you discover what makes you unique. This exercise will help you the most if you are completely honest.

As you think about what your responses will be, go deep. You may hear an answer in your heart or mind and then immediately think, "Oh, I couldn't do that," or, "That would be silly," or, "They'll think I'm ridiculous if I say that." You may even think, "I could never write that down." Your answer may even feel like it is buried deep under the fear that it wouldn't be accepted or that someone would think it's foolish. Don't think about that. You need to

know what YOU think and feel and dream —
regardless of anyone else's opinion. Please don't
give what you think is the politically correct answer;
tell the truth!

That is the focus of this exercise, to reveal
information about you, which you can use to get to
know yourself. Don't forget to answer the WHY part
of the questions.

Please pray this prayer before you start this
wonderful process:

*Father God, I give this time to You, and I'm asking You to
help me hear the truth about myself. Give me the courage to
write down what is truth for me, to really hear the cry of my
own heart. I want to know the person You created me to be,
and I need Your help to identify the blueprint of my life. You
gave me gifts, preferences, likes and dislikes which make me
unique. Help me to know myself and therefore know how You
have anointed me, gifted me and created me.* 5·23·20

In Jesus Name, Amen

Now, as you begin, go to a quiet place and
concentrate on what you hear in your heart. If you
have trouble with some of the questions, place your
hand over your heart, focus on your heart, and just
listen. Remember, God is with you, and He is for
you! Blessings!!

Social Interaction:

The purpose of these questions is to reveal how you interact with others and how much enjoyment you receive from that interaction. Please answer the questions as honestly as you can on a separate piece of paper.

1. Do you prefer peaceful environments or those filled with excitement and action? Why?
2. Do you like parties? Why?
3. Do you like to be around lots of people? Why?
4. Do you like to be alone in nature? Why?
5. Would you rather be indoors or outdoors? Why?
6. Do you prefer to be alone? Why?
7. Would you prefer to discuss a subject with others or think about it alone? Why?
8. Would you prefer to *instruct* someone in how to do something or *show* them how to do something? Why?
9. Do you feel more comfortable acting on an idea or a request, or would you rather think about it and act later? Why?
10. Do you feel comfortable speaking in front of people? Why?
11. Would you prefer to read a book or go to

lunch with a friend? Why?

12. Do you like being with people? Why? (Interaction would entail whether you like being with people. A person might like people, but not like being with them.)

13. What kind of people do you like? Why?

14. What kinds of qualities would you choose in a friend? Why?

15. When you enter a room where a group of people are, can you sense the mood of a group easily? If so, how does that affect you?

16. Are you a sensitive person? If so, does that sensitivity affect how you interact with others? Why?

17. Do you consider yourself a team player? Why?

18. Would you prefer to lead a group or be a part of a group? Why?

19. Will you take charge of a project or a group if there is no distinct leadership? Why?

20. What do you like to do for fun? Does that fun usually include others? Why or why not?

21. What kind of person irritates you? Why?

22. At a social function would you rather be the host, the speaker, the organizer, or clean up after it is over? Why?

23. Do you like to entertain others with jokes? Why?

24. Do you prefer playing games that are solitary, one-on-one, or require team participation? Why?
25. Would you prefer writing a letter to someone or speaking to him/her in person? Why?
26. Do you enjoy having guests in your home? Why?

Personal Preferences:

The purpose of these questions is to reveal your personal preferences and how you would prefer to live your life if money, location, career, etc. were not an issue. Consider how much personal enjoyment is received from experiencing these things, what brings a smile to your face. Please answer the questions as honestly as you can on a separate piece of paper.

1. What is your favorite color? Why?
2. What style of clothing are you most comfortable in? Why?
3. What kind of food do you like to eat? Why?
4. What kind of car do you prefer to drive? Why?
5. If you could live anywhere in the world, where would you live? Why?
6. Where would your most desirable vacation spot be? Why?
7. Do you prefer a neat and orderly environment? Why?
8. Do you prefer to work in a professional environment or a more casual one? Why?
9. Do you prefer a casual lifestyle or one more scheduled? Why?
10. What does a casual/scheduled lifestyle mean to you?

11. What style of furniture do you prefer? Why?
12. How do you feel when friends drop over unannounced? Why?
13. Which style would you choose to decorate your bedroom? Victorian, country, Art Deco, modern, eclectic or something else? Why?
14. Would you like to have a pet? Why?
15. What kind of pet would you have, if you had one? Why?
16. What creates personal value for you? Why?
17. When you consider yourself, what improves your feeling of self-worth? Why?
18. Do you like to wear perfume/aftershave? Why?
19. Do you like to cook, or would you rather eat out? Why?
20. Do you have a special passion for spending time in meditation, soaking prayer or intercessory prayer?
21. What does being a spiritual person mean to you?
22. What does interaction within a church setting mean to you?
23. How important is truth for you personally?
24. How important is truth when you consider that quality in others?
25. Are you an especially playful person?
26. What do you like to do to have fun?
27. Do you enjoy competitive sports such as target-shooting or archery?

28. Do you enjoy leisure activities such as swimming, snow or water skiing, camping, etc. Why?

29. Are you an especially hard worker?

30. What does hard work mean to you?

31. What is success to you? Why?

32. When do you feel the most fulfilled? Why?

33. What excites you? Why?

34. If you could have any job in the world, what would it be? Why?

35. Who do you respect the most? Why?

36. What makes you happy? Why?

37. What irritates you the most? Why?

38. What kind of things do you not like to do? Why?

39. What is the last thing you said "no" to? Why?

40. How would you describe "passion"?

41. What gives you the feeling of "passion"? Why?

42. What do you think is the best stage of life? Why?

43. Do you enjoy children? Why?

44. Would you like to live in a neighborhood with a lot of young families? Why?

45. Do you enjoy solitude? Why?

46. If you could be anyone in the world, living or dead, who would you choose to be? Why?

47. What gives you the greatest joy? Why?

48. Do you like to share your feelings more than most people? Why?
49. How do you prefer to process pain? Why?
50. What did you want to be when you were a child? Why?
51. If there was something you could change about yourself personally, what would it be? Why?
52. If there was something you could change about your life, what would it be? Why?
53. What would bring peace to your life?
54. Would you rather win an award or give an award? Why?
55. Do you enjoy sports? If so, do you enjoy inventing new ways to play?
56. If you enjoy sports, do you enjoy indoor or outdoor sports? Why?

Innate Qualities:

The purpose of these questions is to reveal qualities about you that would not necessarily change when changes in life occur. Innate qualities stay with us and help us to respond to the changes in life, rather than letting the changes in life change us. Please answer the questions as honestly as you can on a separate piece of paper.

1. What qualities do you bring to the table of life
2. What do you like about yourself? Why?

3. What do you consider to be your strengths?
4. How would you describe your personality?
5. Do you love to laugh?
6. Are you self-motivated? Why do you think this is?
7. Are you a goal setter?
8. Do you need goals in your life to move forward? Why?
9. Is stress a motivator or a source of anxiety in your life? Why?
10. What does integrity mean to you?
11. Do you consider yourself a person who has integrity? Why?
12. Do you prefer logic or emotion? Why?

13. Are you drawn to people who are hurting or in pain? Why?

14. How would you describe your character?

15. Are you exceptionally loyal? Why?

16. Do you value loyalty in others? Why?

17. Do you approach life in a focused, organized way? Why?

18. Are you a free spirit? If so, what does that mean to you?

19. Are you spontaneous, or are you methodical, needing to know the next step? Why?

20. When you consider sensitive people, where would you place yourself on the sensitivity spectrum? What things factor in to your assessment?

Creativity:

The purpose of these questions is to reveal qualities about yourself that reflect the enjoyment you get out of life through creative outlets. Please answer the questions as honestly as you can on a separate piece of paper.

1. Do you like to dance or would you prefer watching people dance?
2. What kind of dancing appeals to you?
3. If no one was watching, would you like to dance? Why?
4. Would you like to dance even if someone is watching? Why?
5. Do you enjoy planning parties or events? Why?
6. Is being on stage in a performance something you aspire to? Why?
7. Do you enjoy art? Why?
8. Do you enjoy creating art or viewing art? Why?
9. Do you like to go to concerts? Why?
10. Do you enjoy formal art or abstract? Why?
11. Do you prefer nature scenes or still life? Why?

12. Do you enjoy writing as a form of expression? Why?

13. What is your favorite form of expression?

14. Do you enjoy being a photographer or viewing photography? Why?

15. Is creative cooking something you find fulfilling? Why?

16. Do you enjoy music? Why?

17. What kind of music do you enjoy? Why?

18. Do you like to sing? What does singing do for you?

19. Do you play an instrument? If so, do you still play? Why or why not?

20. What creative endeavor lifts your spirit? Why?

21. What creative endeavor is life-giving to you? Why?

22. Do you enjoy creating things with your hands? What kinds of things do you enjoy creating?

23. Are you mechanical? If so, are you creative in the way you problem-solve, or do you tend to follow the manual?

24. Do you like to come up with new ideas? Why?

25. Do you often find new ways of looking at old ideas? Why?

26. If you are an analytical thinker, do you come up with new insights or perspectives?
27. If you are scientific, do you come up with new theories or possibilities?
28. If you are mathematical, do you find new ways to solve problems?
29. ...*Any* endeavor can be done creatively, whether it be public speaking, managing a store, planning a wedding, arranging furniture, gardening, accounting, etc . If your interests have not been listed here, list them yourself. Then ask yourself, "Do I find my own fresh new ways to accomplish these tasks?

What Don't I Like.....:

The purpose of this section of questions is to help you identify the things in your life that you have given in to, but didn't really want to. This is a short section, but as you answer the questions, if you can think of any more, please feel free to write them down.

1. In the past six months, what have you said yes to that you really wanted to say no to? Why?
2. In the past year, what have you done that would make you look better to a family

member, friend or authority figure that you really didn't want to do? Why?

3. In the past three months, what opinions have you held back from another person rather than being honest? Why?

4. In the past six months, how many times have you felt less valuable because of what someone said to you about *yourself*? Why?

5. In the past six months, how many times has another person been rude or inconsiderate to you and you have chosen to say nothing? Why?

6. In the past three months, have there been any situations that you have withdrawn from or not engaged in because you didn't feel good enough? What made you feel that way? Was it true?

Going Deeper....:

1. What are your spiritual gifts?
2. What kind of character qualities do you have?
3. What is the dream in your heart?
4. What do you value in yourself?
5. What do you value in others?
6. What is your best quality?
7. What do you know about yourself that will never change?
8. What do you need in your life to bring happiness?

9.   What are your values?

Go back and look over the answers that you have given to all these questions. Are there themes that you are noticing, are there ways that you have answered these questions which give meaning to behaviors in your life? As you ponder both the positive questions and the more negative perspective questions, the thing to understand is that the answers you have given on the positive side of things are the preferences, activities and values that bring you life. On the negative side, doing things that we have an aversion to brings us death.

In Deuteronomy 30:19, the Lord told the children of Israel that He had set before them that day life and death, blessing and cursing. He instructed them to choose life. As you look at how you have answered these questions, I would say the same to you. Choose Life! Choose the things that bring you life and stay away from the choices that limit you, make you feel badly and bring you death. Determine how being real to your original design will help you to have a healthier, happier and more purposeful life.

...And now you can answer the most important question,

10. Who are you? Do not answer by telling what you do or with Christian generalities like, "I am a child of God."

Bibliography

American Heritage Dictionary of the English Language, Houghton Mifflin Company, [Boston, MA] 1994

The Amplified Bible, Zondervan, [Grand Rapids, MI] 1983

Purt, Candace B., *Molecules of Emotion: The Science Behind Mind-Body Medicine* [Paperback], Simon & Schuster, [New York, NY] 1999

Childre, Doc, Howard Martin and Donna Beech, *The Heart Math Solution,* Harper Collins, [New York, NY] 2000

The Holy Bible, New King James Version, Thomas Nelson Publishers, [Nashville, TN] 1982

Renner, Rick, *Sparkling Gems from the Greek,* Teach All Nations, [Tulsa, OK] 2003

ABOUT THE AUTHOR

Kriss Mitchell is a Licensed Professional Counselor in the state of Idaho and a Licensed Mental Health Counselor in the state of Washington. She holds certifications in Rehabilitation Counseling, a Doctoral Degree in Natural Health and Board Certification from the International Board of Pastoral and Professional Counselors. Additionally, she has held an appointment as a Domestic Violence Evaluator by the Supreme Court of the state of Idaho, and is an adjunct instructor for the University of Idaho.

As a professional counselor, her areas of specialty include trauma, PTSD, anxiety, identity issues, sexual, spiritual and domestic abuse, addictions, and couples counseling. She also works with individuals who are adult children of Borderline parents or alcoholics. She is trained in EMDR, which is considered the most effective therapy for trauma, and is honored to work with our veterans.

Kriss' approach is gentle, humorous, and compassionate. She believes that it is personal revelation which produces life-changing results. Her belief that unresolved emotional issues are foundational to all personal and physical problems is foundational to the work that she does.

As a teacher, she has a very down-to-earth yet

animated style, connecting with her listeners through humor, powerful examples, and easily applicable truths. Her personal history is one which allows her to empathize with abuse victims, addicts, victims of bullying tactics, and the journey it takes to heal and restore personal value as well as identity. Kriss has been married for 36 years, and has a blended family with four grown children. In addition, she is an accomplished recording artist and enjoys gardening, photography, crafts and travel.

5-19-20

Sympathy is not a solution -
you have to get to the
Root of a problem.

Don't let being a "victim"
become your identity.

He faced the Cross,
focused on the Joy set before Him.
(Heb 12:2)

What we think about + what we say —
+ what we attach emotion to —
we believe.
Those beliefs affect the
electro magnetic resonance around us.